The Wonder of *Believing*

Written by Gregory Hugh Scherrer

Illustrated by Diane Kimble

CrossBooks™
A Division of LifeWay
1663 Liberty Drive
Bloomington, IN 47403
www.crossbooks.com
Phone: 1-866-879-0502

First published by CrossBooks 09/10/2013

ISBN: 978-1-4627-3092-6 (sc)
ISBN: 978-1-4627-3093-3 (e)

Printed in the United States of America.

This book is printed on acid-free paper.

CROSSBOOKS
PUBLISHING

This book is dedicated to my wife DeAnn, my children and their spouses, grandchildren, parents, siblings and the future family that may come my way. God's blessing of family is beyond my ability to describe and I love them all.

I also want to thank my sister Diane Kimble for her work with the illustrations of the book. Her ability to draw the intentions of my heart has been impeccable and I owe to her my thanks and love.

The Wonder of Believing

A story written to encourage parents to be upfront with their children in regards to Santa Claus and the truths of Christ and Christmas. The struggle in the heart of good parents to be honest with their children about these things is real. Great comfort will come as a parent deals with these issues up front. May Christ be honored in all that we do!

Brayla is the special character sharing this story!

The Wonder of Christmas brings with it the spirit of believing.

Many believe in
Santa Claus and
all the attraction
that he draws.

Some
believe
in
Jesus,

He who was the Christ Child!

Christmas time
is so
beautiful
and bright.

It brings great
joy with
every
special sight!

The Lights

The Toys

The Trees

The Joys

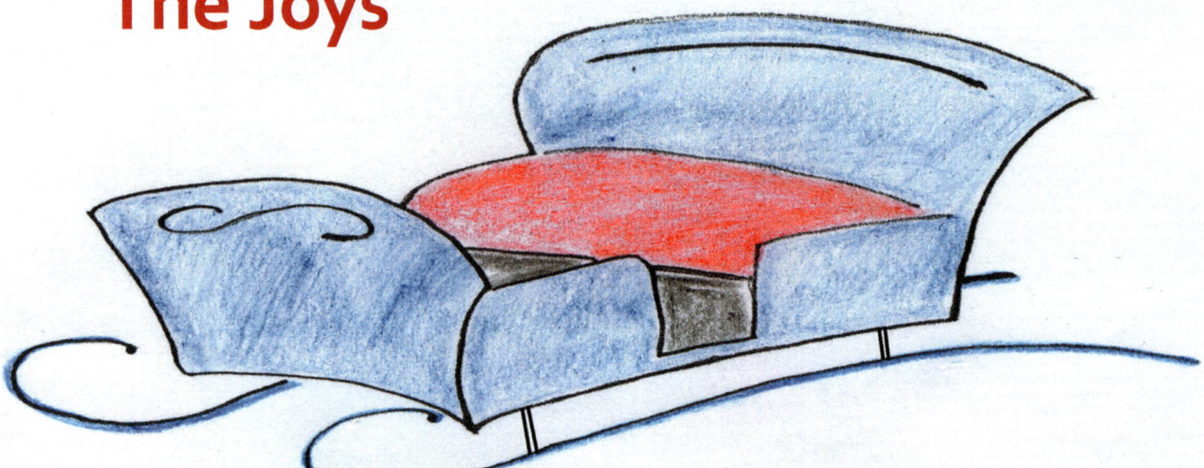

The Food

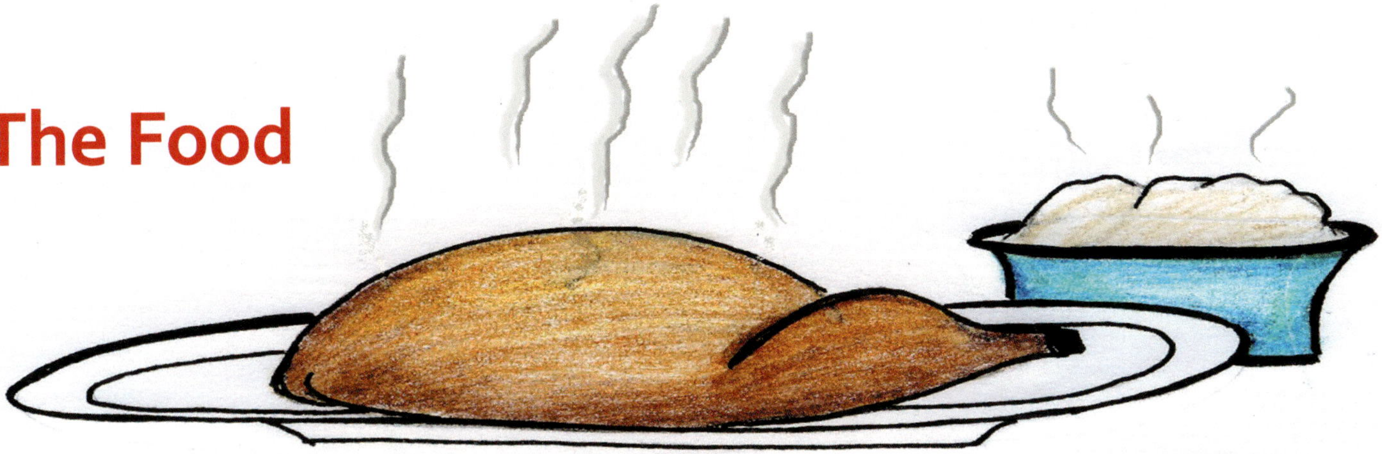

The Crowds

The Stores,
so Loud!

These things they make my heart to swell.

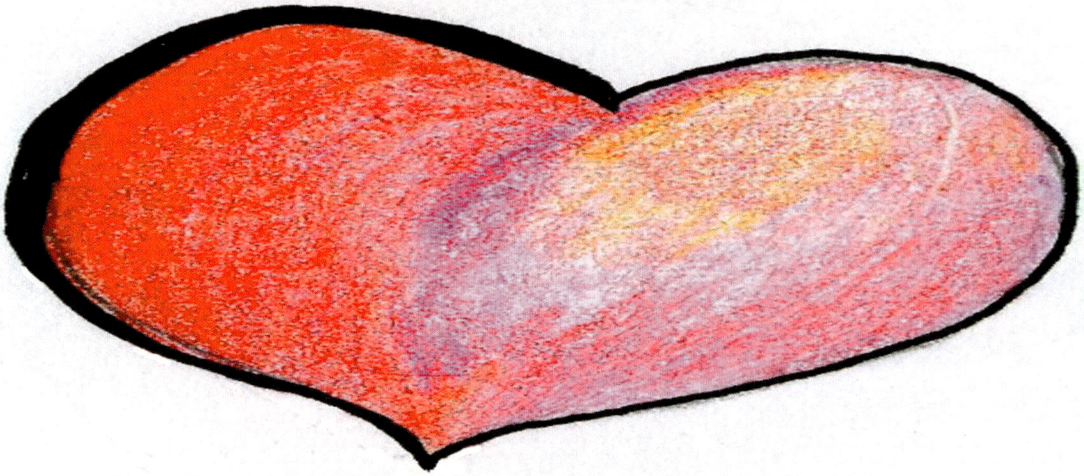

They make me want to

sing

and

yell!

But then I
find my
heart in doubt.

Is this what life is all about?

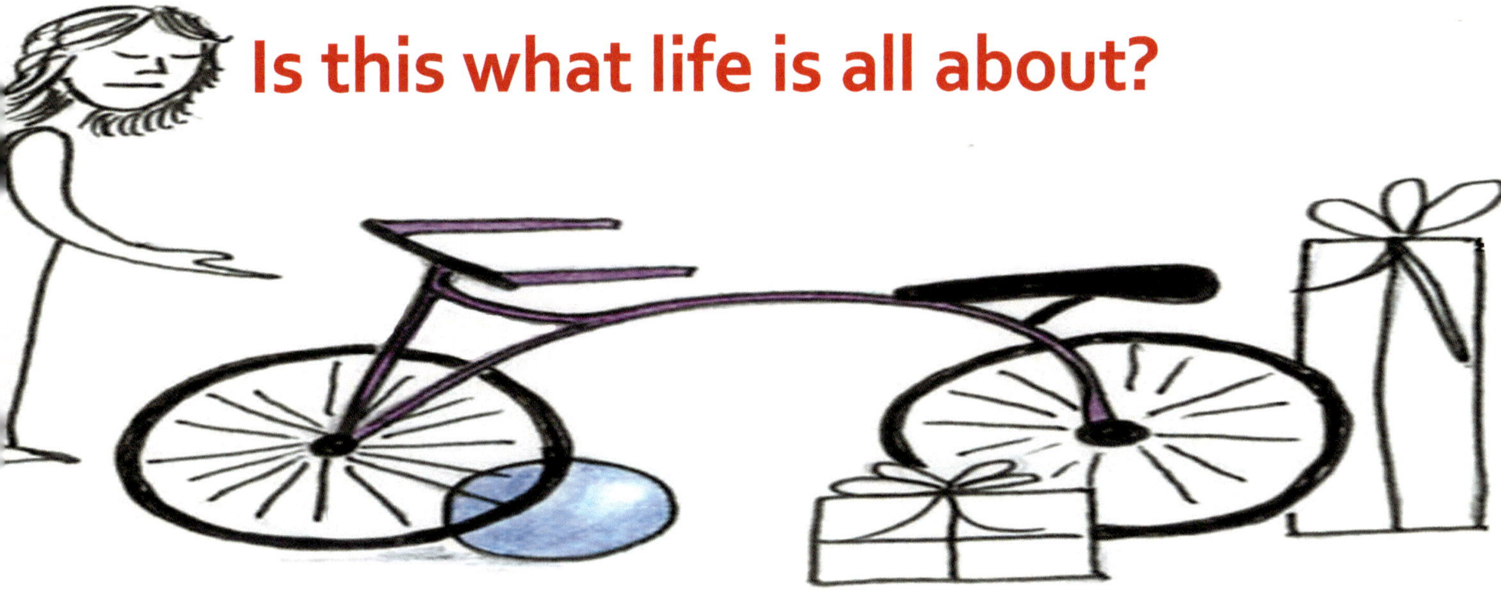

This stuff, these things,

that man whose sleigh makes sleigh bells ring. Is he real?

I knew that all that I had heard
just could not be the final word!

The pain that
came out of
my heart,

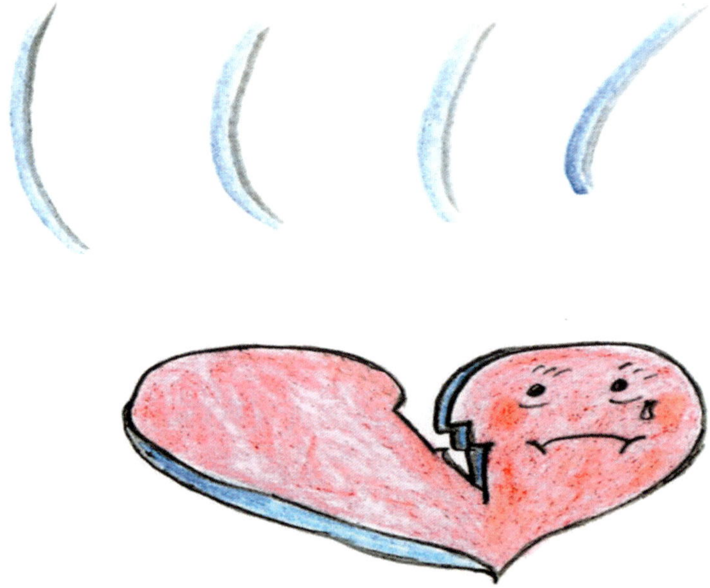

began to take my world apart.

My sin that made life seem so dark,

began to change with
this new spark!

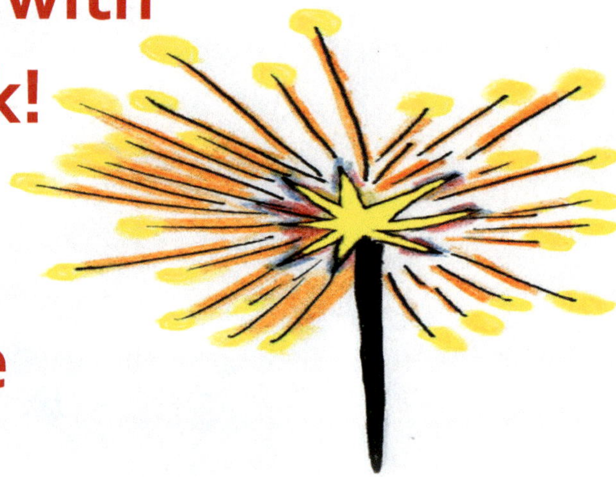

My love of all these
Christmas things,

began to sound a
brand new ring.

The ringing sound
of God's great truth

that brought to
me a
renewed
youth.

Now deep inside my soul I felt

a message burning bright,

that raised my thoughts
to God's good Son
whose life was
given that holy night!

My spirit came to life that day

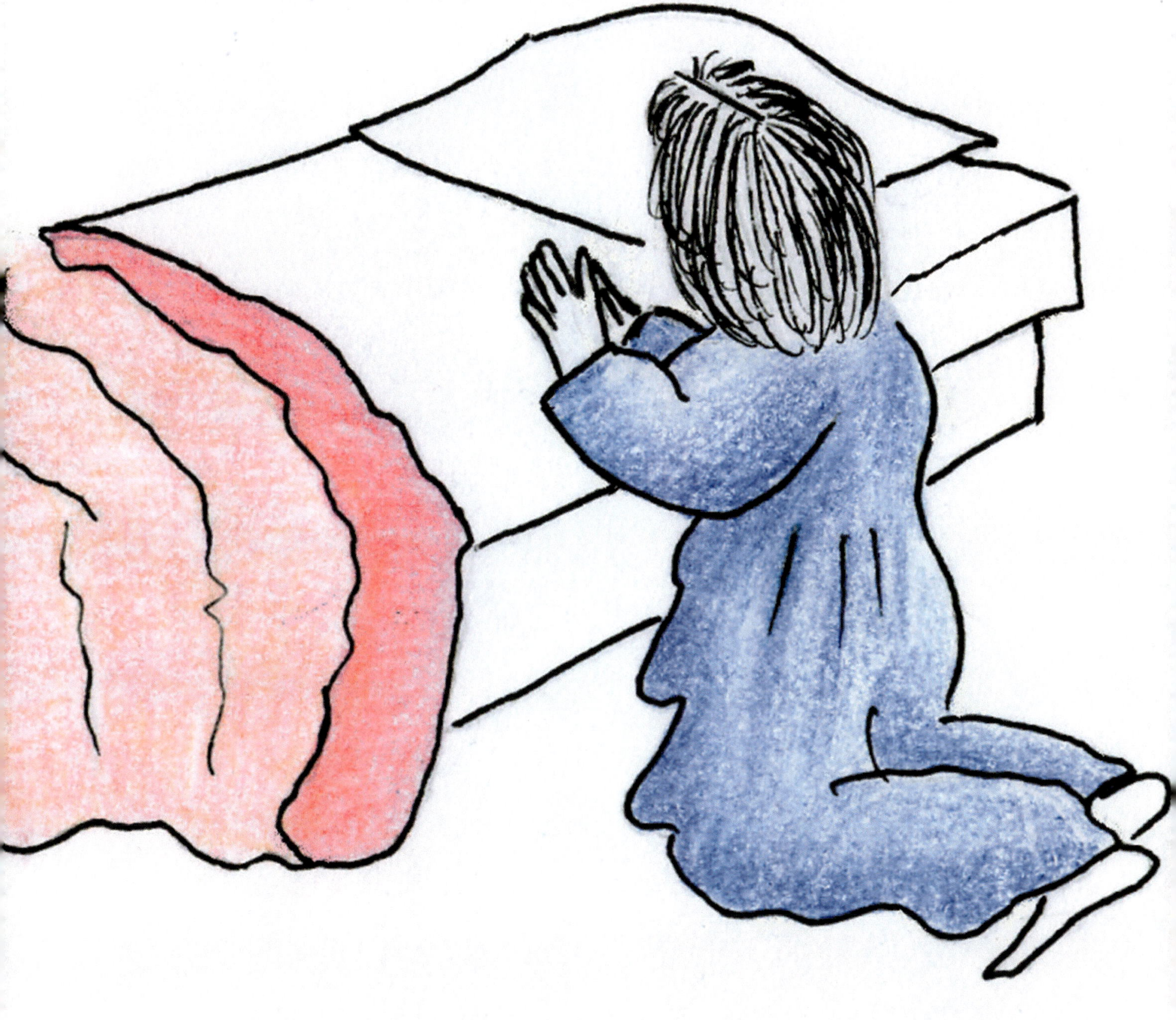

when God Himself
showed me the way.

The path of truth and righteousness,

the road to my heavenly home.

My Savior, Jesus, took my place,
He gave His life for me.

They took Him down that lonely
road to a place called Calvary.

The things I used to love so much
they faded in my view.

Now Santa and that rosy face,
I knew it was not true.

I so much love
this time of year

The lights, the trees
and Christmas cheer.

But now it gives a brand new joy,

because my Savior has come near.

Jesus takes first place!

My God in heaven
has given to me

a new Christmas

Hero!

His name?

Jesus Christ

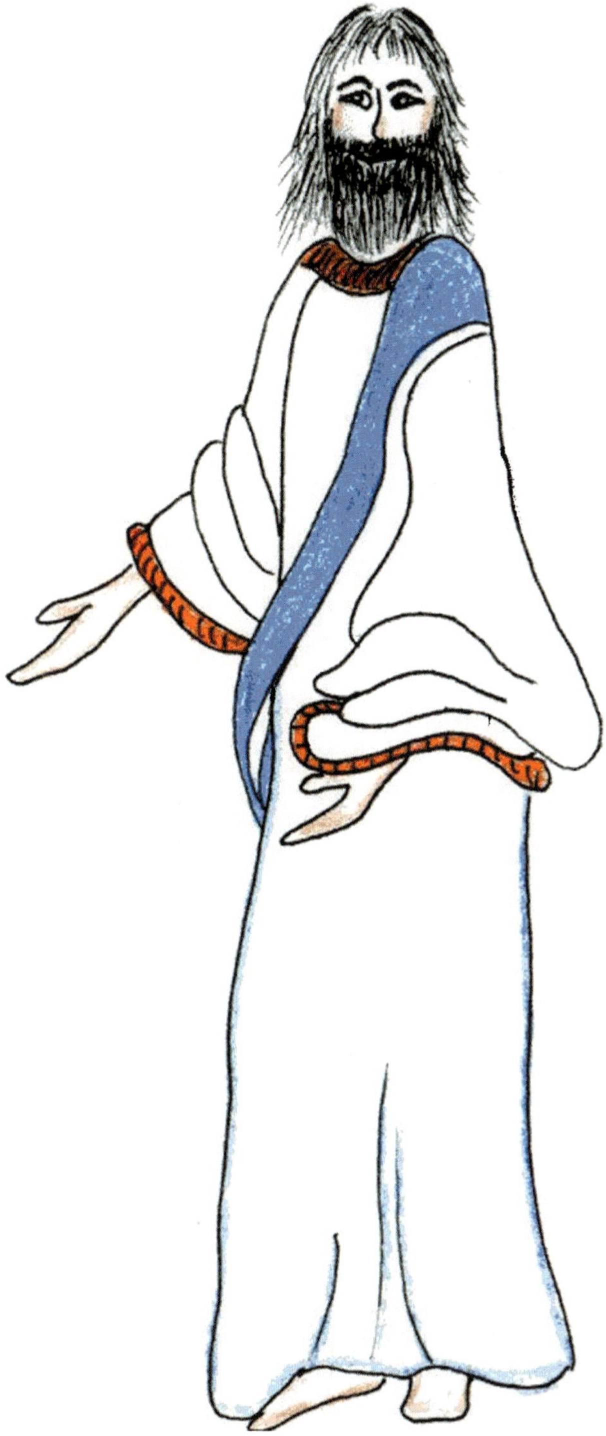

This is the story of
Christ my Savior!

Do You Believe in Jesus?

Place your picture in the square
if you trust Jesus like I do.

TOOK MY PLACE!

Author
Greg Scherrer

Greg Scherrer is the Pastor of Hi-Plains Baptist Church of Limon, Colorado and teaches music in the local public school. He and his wife, DeAnn, came to know Christ as Savior in January of 1991 and they give thanks to God for the changes granted to them. This book is written in the hope that Christian families would use some of the secular traditions of Christmas as stepping stones for sharing Christmas truth with their kids. Parent's struggle with what to do with Santa Claus; many embrace his existence fully until their children learn otherwise while others put him up on the shelf of worldly evils as their children watch him sit on that shelf for years as they wonder. The "Wonder of Believing" will give parents a tool to use early in their Child's life as they share the gospel through the stories and traditions of Christmas. Pastor Scherrer's hope is that parents use this story to step squarely into the truth of sin and God's provision for that sin. May your children be enthralled with the grace and wonder of Jesus Christ!

CPSIA information can be obtained
at www.ICGtesting.com
Printed in the USA
LVIC04n0017240913
353814LV00002B
9781462730926